SAP SRM Interview Questions, Answers, and Explanations

By Jim Stewart

Please visit our website at www.srmcookbook.com

The programs in this book have been included for instructional value only. They have been tested with care but are not guaranteed for any particular purpose. The publisher does not offer any warranties or representations not does it accept any liabilities with respect to the programs.

Trademark notices

SAP, SAP EBP, SAP SRM, Netweaver, and SAP New Dimension are registered trademarks of SAP AG. This publisher gratefully acknowledges SAP permission to use its trademark in this publication. SAP AG is not the publisher of this book and is not responsible for it under any aspect of the law.

Motivation

During the course of an average project, I am usually called upon by a project manager to "help screen resources" for different parts of the project. And one thing comes to mind – if done properly, it's very time consuming, and it's really hard work!

My interviews usually sound something like this –

Jim: "Please rate yourself, on a scale of 1-10 on your SRM knowledge and experience..."

Interviewee: "Um, probably something like 10..."

Jim: "OK, so, let me just say something... I don't believe there is such a thing as a ten."

Interviewee: "What would you rate yourself?"

Jim: "I rate myself an 8."

Interviewee: "Why so low?"

Jim: "There's no such thing as a ten. All of the nines are working at SAP, SAP Labs, or SAP Consulting, and so basically that puts me at about an eight. But we're here to talk about **your** skills. And so you think you're a 10, huh? OK, so tell me what you know about debugging the n-step approval workflow..."

And then I try to ask the questions that truly flesh out a person's understanding of the software. It's part science, part art to be sure – but the #1 thing I'm looking for in an interview is that the resource represents their skills truthfully. The good resources know what they know, know what they don't know, and they're open about it.

And so I hope that this book will serve as a much-needed guide for managers trying to get the right resource for their project. If you construct an interview based on these questions, I'm confident you can get a good idea about the depth and breadth of a consultant's experiences and accumulated knowledge.

Jim Stewart

Detroit, Michigan

August 2005

Introduction

This book is divided into three parts – configuration related questions, technical and troubleshooting questions, and finally, strategy and strategic purchasing questions.

Each interview question has a question and an answer – that is pretty straightforward – but when you see the guru icon – this is information that represents the highest degree of knowledge in a particular area. So if you're looking for a "workflow guru" be sure to listen for an answers similar to those given under the guru icon.

Don't be bamboozled!

The SRM Guru has Spoken!

Part I: Configuration Related Questions

Question 1: Name some of the Basis Steps associated with the configuration of SRM.

A: Maintain Logical System for both the EBP client and R/3 client that EBP will be connected to in the EBP golden client as well as in the R/3 golden client. Use transaction SM59.

Create System users for running standard EBP reports and for Workflow Processing. Use transaction SU01.

Maintain RFC Destination for both the EBP client and R/3 client that EBP will be connected to in the EBP connected as well as in the R/3 connected client.

Activate the Standard Workflow Customizing using transaction SWU3 (especially the synchronization of the WF-BATCH user ID and password)

Set the exit URL for the ITS to the SRM login page, schedule standard system reports, enable English language on ITS login page.

Question 2: Why do you configure number ranges in SRM?

A: Number ranges must be established for EBP shopping carts as well as any potential purchasing document so that unique numbers can be generated in the backend R/3 system from EBP.

When a shopping cart is submitted to R/3, a requisition, reservation, purchase order or service order will be generated. The EBP system needs a number range established that automatically takes the next available number and assigns it to the document which will be created in R/3. Configuration must also be established in the R/3 system to correlate with the ranges setup in EBP so that a conflict never arises when a purchasing document is created directly in the R/3 system on a similar number range. This configuration is covered in a separate document.

Question 3: What is the relationship between an SRM Vendor List and an R3 Source List?

A: Vendor lists in EBP are completely separate from traditional source lists in the R/3 backend system and must be setup on their own internal number range in the EBP system.

Question 4: What number ranges must be configured in SRM?

A: Entries should be created in the EBP system to link the EBP purchase orders, requisitions and reservations to the backend R/3 system. PO, RQ and RS were used to easily distinguish each number range defined in the next section. The logical system ID should reflect that of the EBP application server and client in which the number ranges are being configured.

Question 5: Why do you create the internal number range for local bid invitations?

A: An internal number range must be defined to numerically build local bid invitations for RFQ's and Auctions in the Bidding Engine and Live Auction applications. These bids do not have a link to any R/3 purchasing documents, they are completely local to the EBP system.

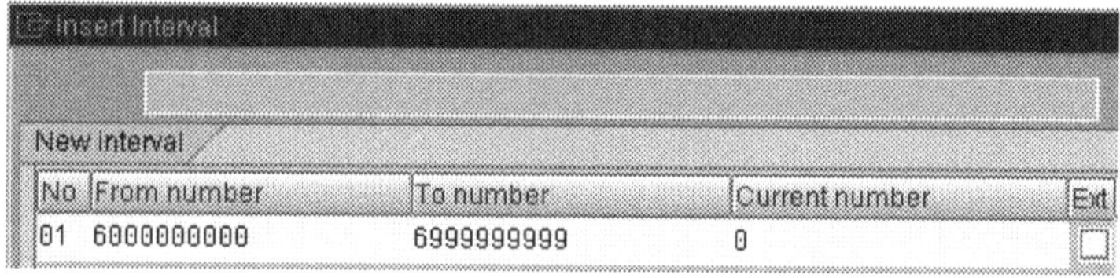

Question 6: How do you define the ITS URL?

A: Transaction: SM30
Table: TWPURLSVR

Before the Internet Transaction Server can process EBP requests, entries in table TWPURLSVR must be maintained to initiate a connection to a physical URL. This URL controls the menu on the left hand side of the screen that houses all of the transactions users have access to.

The URL will vary depending on which EBP client the configuration is performed in. The URL should consist of base address for the Integrated ITS instance. This configuration should only need to be performed once for each client in which EBP purchasing will be enabled.

Fill in the ITS host and port numbers for the first 2 server entries and tag the protocols as 'http':

Question 7: What is the SRM equivalent of an R3 MM Material Group?

A: Product Category

Question 8: If you only want to replicate a subset of material groups to SRM product categories, how is this accomplished?

A: Set Filter to Exclude Material Groups

Use Transaction: R3AC3 on customizing object: DNL_CUST_PROD1

Filters can set to include or exclude specific product categories (material groups) from being replicated over to the EBP system from the R/3 system. We will replicate only the UNSPSC codes selected for this example configuration. All others will be excluded. These entries are not transportable because they are directly tied to the R/3 client specified by the Site Name chosen for the filter. When the filter is generated in the EBP system, the filter settings are transferred to a table in the R/3 client so when new categories are created or existing ones are changed, the R/3 system knows which records to consider for replication.

Question 9: In the Disconnected mode, how many local systems should be defined?

A: Only one system can be indicated as the local system.

Question 10: How often must you define the address of an org unit?

A: Each org unit should always have an address maintained. In this example the corporate address was maintained. This address will most likely never be used, as users will probably be attached to lower levels of the org structure. Regardless, in the rare event that this address may be adopted as a delivery address, a realistic address should be specified.

Question 11: Is there anything special about replicating vendors in the org plan?

A: Once the Root organizational unit is created, you must create a special org unit for vendors which can be accessed from transaction PPOMA_BBP.

Maintain the an address for the organizational unit. Each org unit should always have an address maintained. In this example the corporate address was maintained. This address should never be used in transaction processing.

Question 12: What are some of the non-MM objects that must be replicated into the SRM system?

A: This will include data such as product categories, currency conversion rates, and units of measure.

Question 13: If you are replicating from the backend and something is stuck in the queue in R/3, what can you do?

A: Use transaction SMQ1 (in R/3)

The first thing that should be checked when downloading customizing objects is a possible stuck queue. The EBP system primarily uses the Inbound queue (SMQ2) whereas the R/3 system uses the Outbound queue (SMQ1). The outbound queue is more often than not the queue that gets stuck initially.

Question 14: What can you do to see if you have a stuck Queue in EBP?

A: Run transaction SMQ2 (EBP).

If the Outbound queue was stuck in Section C, then most likely the Inbound queues in EBP are waiting to be manually activated.

Question 15: **Is there anything in particular that needs to be done to a user or vendor to make them a valid part of SRM?**

A: A user or supplier record cannot be assigned to an organizational unit until it has a business partner record generated.

Explanation: When Business Partner relationships are not established, users cannot be imported into the organizational structure from the Users_Gen transaction. The following error results:

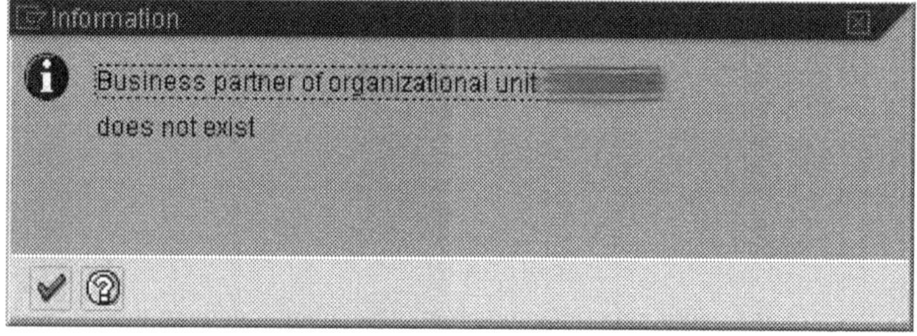

Question 16: What purpose does the SRM org structure serve?

A: Organizational attributes serve many purposes in the EBP system. The primary purpose is to set attributes that define the users experience when shopping. Some example attributes are company codes, plants and cost centers that a user can order against.

Question 17: What are some of the most important attributes assigned in the org structure, and what are their purposes?

A: Accounting System Alias (ACS)

Set reference accounting system for account assignment element reference.

A: Backend Document Type (BSA)

The BSA (document type in R/3 system) organizational attribute links an EBP shopping cart to a document type in R/3 for purchase requisitions and purchase orders in R/3. A single document type 'ECPO' should be defined in the R/3 client which the EBP system is connected to by the MM team. This is the value that should be defined for the backend document type preceeded by the logical system and a backslash.

With this value set, any requisitions or purchase order generated in R/3 from EBP shopping carts will be tied to document type ECPO.

A: Company Code (BUK)

This Local attribute definition for company code is the key to defining allowable delivery addresses for a given location. In order for users to have the ability to look up addresses from a list, this attribute must be set and the "Edit Internal Addresses" transaction must be used to create the list.

A: Movement Type Attribute (BWA)

It is necessary to maintain the attribute if the default material group for a given user or site is set to a backend logical system. The EBP system knows that if the user is set for backend procurement, that there might be a possibility for a reservation to be generated, therefore it checks to see that a value for this attribute is maintained. The BWA value should be defined for the as 201 preceeded by the logical system and a backslash.

A: Local Currency Attribute (CUR)

The local currency controls what currency the requisitioners see their shopping cart pricing in. If a catalog item is pulled in that is not equal to their local currency attribute, the currency will be converted in the EBP system using the conversion rates replicated over from the R/3 system (which are actually published from MONEX or other conversion application). The local currency is an important attribute in driving approval processes to trigger for the local spend and approval limits per region.

Question 18: What is the purpose of the Forward Work Item Attribute (FORWARD_WI)?

A: It controls notification of work items for each user in the org plan.

The forward work item attribute when flagged, automatically sends approval notifications from the user's SAP inbox to their Outlook (or other external) mailbox. According to the Global key decisions defined, this attribute should be set to forward all work items. The exclusion checkbox can be used to stop the forwarding if necessary for a given user or group of users.

Question 19: What is the significance of the product category in SRM?

A: The product category drives which system purchase requisitions; purchase orders, contracts, goods receipts, invoices, and contracts eventually flow into. This configuration is required for each product category before a user can order with the category.

There are two ways this configuration can be setup. Each category can be configured separately or a * can be used to denote that all categories follow the same path. Unless there are plans to stray from the Classic EBP mode to De-coupled or Standalone or there are plans to integrate multiple R/3 backend instances, a * is recommended to denote all categories are designated to the single R/3 backend system.

ID of the backend R/3 system for both the Source System and Target System fields. Since the categories were replicated from R/3 to EBP, the source and the target are one in the same.

Question 20: How do you make the catalog link appear for a user?

A: Catalog call structures must be defined in the EBP system to enable links to display in the Catalog tab of the shopping cart to both internal and external catalogs.

Only internal catalogs will be covered in this chapter

Question 21: Do vendors exist in the SRM system, or do you use the backend vendors?

A: Vendor master records must be replicated over to EBP from R/3 before a user can access the vendor from their shopping cart. When in Classic mode, vendor master records remain parent records in the R/3 system, the EBP records simply act as child records. There is some data that can be extended on a vendor master record in the EBP system that the R/3 system either does not replicate over or does not have available, otherwise all other data is overwritten when a subsequent replication is run.

GURU: Once a vendor has been replicated over to the EBP system from the R/3 system, all changes to that master record in R/3 can only be synchronized in the EBP system through transaction BBPUPDVD.

Question 22: **What is the TCODE used to replicate vendors from the backend to SRM?**

Transaction: BBPGETVD

Question 23: How do you know if a shopping cart will generate a PR or PO?

A: There are two ways this configuration can be setup. Each category can be configured separately or a * can be used to denote that all categories follow the same path. Unless there are plans to stray from the Classic EBP mode to De-coupled or Standalone or there are plans to integrate multiple R/3 backend instances, a * is recommended to denote all categories are designated to the single R/3 backend system.

In the EBP Classic mode, once a shopping cart is approved, an option exists to either generate a purchase requisition, purchase order or a reservation based on the information available in the shopping cart line items.

Question 24: How do you control which catalogs a user sees?

A: Catalog views are assigned to the users through the CAT organizational attribute. This attribute value is case-sensitive, ensure the catalog ID is entered as it is configured in the system.

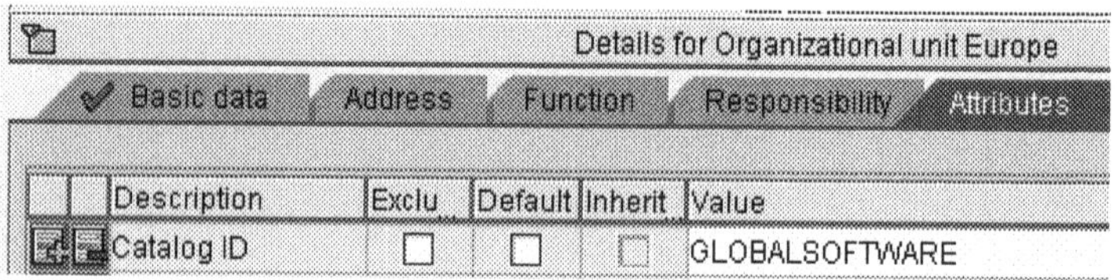

Question 25: How can you automate vendor replication in SRM?

A: In the EBP system, an automated vendor replication job and update job can be activated automatically in the IMG to eliminate the need to periodically manually retrieve new vendor master records or vendor master record updates.

Question 26: How does SRM maintain sychronization with the backend R/3 system?

A: There are two jobs that maintain the status of shopping carts in SRM.

The CLEAN_REQREQ_UP and BBP_GET_STATUS2 jobs will be configured to run in each EBP client to synchronize status data between EBP and R/3. The following are recommended intervals will be setup within the respective EBP clients. These values are subject to change over time if performance becomes an issue or the intervals are set too far apart and performance has not been an issue.

CLEANER JOB: The cleaner job was created by SAP to delete unnecessary (obselete) data/records in the EBP system after verification that all order data was successfully posted in the R/3 system. For example, when a purchase order is successfully posted in R/3, the cleaner job will delete temporary shopping cart table records that are no longer necessary in EBP since the master record of the order shifts to the R/3 system in de-coupled mode.

A: STATUS JOB: The status job was created by SAP to update the EBP system with data such as purchase requisition number, purchase order number, goods received or invoices recorded manually in R/3, etc. The report should not be run on a frequent basis at short intervals unless the order count from EBP to R/3 is not that high. Otherwise, a recommended interval for running the report is approximately every hour. Until this job runs, the user will not see the number of the backend document created in R/3 for a particular shopping cart in the history tab of the check status transaction.

Question 27: Can tax calculation be disabled?

A: The EBP system allows several avenues for calculating tax for shopping cart line items, including no tax calculation.

In transaction SPRO follow menu path: SAP Implementation Guide → Supplier Relationship Management → SRM Server → Cross-Application Basic Settings → Tax Calculation → Determine System for Tax Calculation

Select the radio button for "No Tax Calculation":

Defining System for Tax Calculation

System for tax calculation	Choose
No Tax Calculation	◉

Click on the button to save the configuration.

Question 28: Why would I mark the standard approval workflows as a general task?

A: The standard workflows delivered by the system all have the "No general task" setting applied. Unless roles are attached to the workflow to determine who can and cannot process a particular workflow, then no one can process the workflow. Therefore the Workflow Templates should be converted to "General Task" so they can be used. Individual approval tasks may or may not be set with "General Task".

This is a one time configuration step for each time a new SRM instance is implemented.

Question 29: What is the purchasing organization hierarchy?

The Purchasing Organization hierarchy comprises Company Codes, Purchasing Organizations, Plants and Purchasing Groups.

Question 30: What is a Company Code?

A: A Company Cody is its own **legal entity** within SAP with its own Balance Sheet and Profit and Loss account and forms part of the your Corporate Group.

Question 31: What is a Purchasing Organization?

A: A **Purchasing Organization** is the organizational unit within a business that is responsible for the procurement of goods and services for plants that fall within a particular region. The Purchasing Organization also negotiates terms and conditions of contracts and purchases from vendors and assumes legal responsibility for these purchases for the Plants that the Purchasing Organization is responsible for. The Plants that a Purchasing Organization is responsible for is dependant on its assignment.

Question 32: What is the purpose of a Plant?

A: A **Plant** is an operational unit within an organization and has its own address, language, country and master data. A Plant is assigned to Purchasing Organization in the Implementation Guide (IMG) and the Purchasing Organization then assumes the roles and activities involved in the procurement of goods and services described above for that Plant.

Question 33: What is the purpose of a Purchasing Group?

A: Purchasing groups are further sub-divisions of the Purchasing Organization and are responsible for the day-to-day buying activities. Typically a Purchasing Group can be seen as a single buyer or group of buyers responsible for purchasing activities. A Purchasing Group is not assigned to a single Purchasing Organization or Plant and is able to carry out buying activities across these structures.

Question 34: What is the middleware used for?

A: Middleware Setup to make data transfer possible to the EBP system.

Middleware is used on the R/3 application to transfer and synchronize master data between other SAP instances such as Enterprise Buyer Professional and Supplier Self Services. Example master data includes plants, commodity codes, material master records, etc.

This initial setup of middleware described in this document should only need to be processed in a new SRM client or re-validated when a client copy, system refresh or the existing backend system client is swapped out with a new or other client.

Question 35: How do you define the logical System for Initial Downloads

A: Use Transaction: SM30
Table: CRMRFCPAR
Transport: Not Transportable

Create entries in table CRMRFCPAR in the backend R/3 system for initial and delta downloads using the logical system name of the EBP client in which replication exchange will take place.

These entries must be manually created in each new EBP client connected to an R/3 backend system, as the correct logical system must be populated in the Destination field.

Question 36: What is the purpose of a document type? How does this apply to a PR? To a PO?

A: SAP uses Document Types to group documents with similar characteristics together. **Purchase Requisitions** are grouped together depending on, firstly, where they originate from and secondly, by what type of purchasing document they will become. The number range is assigned to that particular document type enabling SAP to create Purchase Requisitions from a particular Number Range. For the Source to Pay project all requisitions will be generated from the Enterprise Buyer Professional front-end, therefore a new document type has to be configured and the number range assigned to this Document Type in the SAP R/3 system has to agree with the number range for Purchase Requisitions in the SRM system.

Purchase Orders are similarly grouped together by document type depending on the PO characteristics. PO's for the S2P project will be initiated from the EBP front-end and as such all PO's will have the item category ECPO.

For the S2P project the Document Type ECPO is linked to relevant Purchasing Item Categories and assigned the correct number range. In the case of Purchase Requisitions, this number range should be identical to the EBP Shopping Cart Number Range.

Question 37: How are product categories represented in R3?

A: Commodity Codes and SRM Product Categories are identified in SAP as Material Groups. Material Groups are maintained to group together materials that have the same characteristics or are used for similar purposes and enable analyses and search functionality.

Part II: Technical and Troubleshooting Questions

Question 38: What are some of the most important SRM programs?

A: Shopping Cart Creation — Program SAPBBPPU99, Service BBPPU99

Account Assignment — Function group BBP_PDH_ACC, Service BBPACCOUNT

Approval work item web transaction — Program SAPMTS1 0008069H, Service TS_TS10008069H

Shopping Cart Status — Program SAPBBPPU02, Service BBPPU02

Login and launch pad — Program SAPBBPST01, Service BBPSTART

Shared MIME / JavaScript / HTML Business / Java Applet files — service BBPGLOBAL

Confirmations (Goods Receipt) — Function group BBP_CF, Service BBPCF02

Question 39: Can you add a new attribute to the organizational plan?

A: Yes. Use transaction SM30 to add entries to table T770MATTR.

The attribute must first be created in the attributes section. This includes linking the attribute with a data dictionary type definition, and determining whether multiple values are permissible or whether local values should override inherited values. Customer specific attributes must start with Z.

Once the attribute has been created, include the attribute in the EBP scenario, and assign the 0 (organizational unit) and S (position) object types to the attribute to allow it to be assigned to org units/positions on the organizational plan.

The attributes can then be accessed via transaction PPOMA_BBP in the same way as standard SAP attributes.

Question 40: How do you open extra fields in the account assignment screens?

A: Use transaction SM30 to add entries to table BBP_C_ACCF.

This table determines which fields are open for display/change in the extended account assignment screens. For each account category, only one field must be marked as the main field. More fields can be added as secondary fields to be opened. To find the field names, examine the field list of screen 2000 of function group BBP_PDH_ACC.

Question 41: What are some of the most popular workflows in the SRM system? Are there any variati ons?

A: The most frequently deployed workflows are the shopping cart approval workflows.

Several approval workflows are provided as examples. These are working examples that can be used as-is if desired. Many customers do use them as-is, particularly for pilots. The main workflows are:

WS 10000060— No approval (i.e. automatic approval)

WS 10000129 — One step approval (approval by manager, i.e. chief position in same org unit).

WS 10000031 — Two step approval (first approval is by manager, second approval is by manager's manager)

WS 10000276 — Spending limit approval (approval is by nominated approval manager for the relevant approval limit, based on the total value of the shopping cart)

WS1000133 – n-step approval with BADI

There are also workflows for confirmations (goods receipts) and invoices.

Question 42: How do you copy a workflow for modification?

A: Use transaction PFTC_COP to copy workflows.

To change the copied workflows use transaction PFTCCHG.

Changing Workflows

Use transaction PFTCCHG to change workflows.

You should only change your own copies — never change the standard workflows.

When changing any shopping cart approval workflow be careful how you affect the applet for the approval display in the "Check Status" (BBPPUO2) web transaction. Any steps you add that should NOT appear in the display should have the flag "step not in workflow log" turned on in the workflow step. This flag removes the step from the graphical workflow log, which is the source of the data for the approval display. The step can still be seen in the technical view of the log so that a workflow administrator can resolve any problems.

Start Conditions

Start conditions are accessible from the IMG. Transaction SWBPROCTJREMENT.

The start condition editor enables:

a) Activation/deactivation of triggering event linkage to workflows

b) Creation/change/deletion of logical expression to act as start condition

The check function module SWB CHECK PB START COND EVAL evaluates the start condition. Therefore start conditions are only relevant if the check function module has been included in the event type linkage (accessed via transaction SWETYPV) of the triggering event/workflow in question (this situation may change in later releases — it's likely that checking of start conditions will be automatic for all workflows).

The logical expression can be based on:

Constants — e.g. $500

Workflow system elements — e.g. workflow initiator

Object attributes — e.g. "requisitioner" of shopping cart

Customer-specific object attributes can be used.

The key point to remember in creating the logical expression is that only values known at event creation time can be used. For instance, approver could NOT be used as this is not known until after the workflow has started.

Creating new object attributes

Create a subtype of the standard SAP business object type (transaction SW01).

The subtype must start with Z, and the subtype program must start with Z.

Change status of subtype to "implemented" and then to "released".

Generate the subtype.

Use system-wide delegation to delegate the SAP business object type to the new subtype.

Create new attributes on the subtype.

Implement the matching code in the subtype program as necessary and regenerate.

When creating new attributes for a subtype of BUS2 121 (Requirement Coverage Request, alias the shopping cart), be careful that you cater for both an existing shopping cart and a temporary shopping cart. If you don't cater for the temporary shopping cart and you use these attributes in start conditions or agent determination the approval preview will fail or fail to show the correct approvers. To understand how to access the temporary shopping cart make sure you look at the programming underneath the standard BUS2 121 program (mostly this is done by using IMPORT FROM MEMORY to read the temporary structures output by the shopping cart program SAPBBPPU99).

Options for creating new role resolutions

The full SAP Business Workflow environment is available. This gives the following options for new role resolutions:

• Standard role based on "responsibilities" created via transaction PFAC. This allows input criteria to be specified as role container elements. Possible input criteria combinations (which may include ranges and/or lists of single values) are then defined as responsibility areas, and agents assigned to the responsibility areas. It is also possible to assign "priorities" to the responsibility criteria combinations. This allows certain criteria to be assessed prior to others, e.g. look for a specific match, if not found, assess more general entries. Criteria with higher priorities are assessed before lower priorities, highest priority is 99, and lowest priority is 1.

NOTE: Essentially this is equivalent to creating a customer table of criteria combinations mapped against agents, which could then be evaluated by a customer specific role function module. However responsibility roles do not require further programming, so it is recommended that they be used in place of customer tables.

Standard role based on a customer specific role function module created via transaction PFAC. This may be useful in complex situations. For instance, where agents need to be determined based on information in the backend R/3 system. One example, determining the cost centre manager from fields in the cost centre master data in the backend R3 system. Any agents determined must be mapped to valid EBP organizational units/positions or to valid EBP userids.

There are other mechanisms available (e.g. SAP organizational object assignment or SAP office distribution lists) however the above two methods are the most useful within the context of EBP.

Including new role resolutions in Ad hoc agent assignment

Ad hoc agent assignment has two major purposes within EBP.

1. It allows the default approvers to be calculated at the commencement of the workflow so that current and future approvers can be displayed as part of shopping cart status and the approval workitem.

2. Through coding in the shopping cart status and approval workitem programs, the change approver function can be used to change the selected agent dynamically.

To include role resolutions in ad hoc agent assignment, the following steps are needed.

1. Create a subtype of standard SAP business object type AAGENT to represent the new role.

2. Use code in standard object type ASBMANAGER as a template for code in new subtype.

3. Redefine and change the code in the "Create" method of the new subtype to determine the default approver as needed. This involves firstly determining the input criteria, e.g. by evaluating attributes of object references in the approval workflow container, then evaluating the new role resolution. If a responsibility role was created, function module RH can be called to evaluate the role. Otherwise, the role function module itself is called at this point. The list of agents must be resolved down to user names for EBP. Function module RH_STRUC_GET can be used to do this (see coding example in function module SWX_GET_MANAGER).

4. In the "Create" method, don't forget to check whether the shopping cart is temporary or existing. If temporary, you will need to send the list of agents to a container element called "Agents", otherwise the agent list will not display on the approval preview. The program code underneath the "Create" method for the standard business object ASBMANAGER shows how to do this.

5. Create the new workflow either via shopping cart approval wizard or as a copy of one of the existing approval workflows. In the workflow container, set up an approver container element referencing the new subtype. In the approval step, assign the "Agents" attribute of the approver container element as the responsible agent.

At runtime, an initial step (or basic data of the workflow definition in later releases) of the workflow runs the "Execute" method of the "Ad hoc factory" object. This step instantiates all workflow container elements that reference object type AAGENT or any of its subtypes, and executes the relevant "Create" method to determine the default approver. That is, at this point the default approvers are calculated so that they can be shown in the shopping cart status display, and in all approval workitems.

The default approver determined in the "Create" method becomes the selected agent of the approval step, providing of course that they are also possible agents of the approval task.

Possible agents of the approval workflow have the authority to change the approver either via the shopping cart status (for the requisitioner), or via the approval workitem (for reviewers/approvers — e.g. to change subsequent approvers). The code to change the agent has been directly coded into the programs behind shopping cart status and the web transaction for the approval workitem.

The change approver function allows the user to change the selected agent of the approval workitem to another possible agent. Therefore, the change approver function is only relevant when the approval task has been assigned to specific possible agents (e.g. via security roles [activity groups]) and NOT to general task.

Note that forwarding the workitem to another possible agent has the same effect as changing the approver at the current approval level — so workflow administrators can redirect these workitems via SAPGUI and do not need to go out to the web to do this.

Workitems via the web

All standard tasks to be performed via the web have:

- Object type FORM and method HTMLPROCESS
- A link to a generated web transaction (via menu path GOTO → Web Transaction) program
- ITS service/template files matching the web transaction program

The generated web transaction program consists of four (4) main screens:

- Screen 50— Entry screen for pickup of the workitem id
- Screen 100 — Main screen for execution of the workitem
- Screen 150— Main screen for start of a workflow (NOT USED IN EBP)
- Screen 200 — Confirmation messages screen

In addition some web transactions have been significantly changed from the original generated web transaction. For example, the web transaction for the shopping cart approval uses screen 100 as a main screen to call a number of subscreens to display all the approval information from the approval workitem.

Note that several standard tasks may be connected to the same web transaction. For instance, a number of separate but similar standard tasks link to the web transaction for shopping cart approval. This enables different possible agent assignment per standard task, but consistency of the approval workitem operation.

Question 43: How does SRM handle email notification?

A: In EBP, program RSWUWFMLEC is used to create email notifications of outstanding work items. This program is a variant of the standard R3 email notification program

RSWUWFML.

The following pre-conditions must be met before email notifications can be sent:

a) EBP system must be configured to be able to send email to an Internet email address via the appropriate mail server. That is, SAP Connect or SMTP or similar must be installed between EBP and the mail server.

b) An email address must be assigned to the workflow system user (i.e. user id WF-BATCH) as the sender address. This email address must be acceptable to the mail server, i.e. not produce an error when it is used as the sender address. Transaction SWU3 is used to assign the email address to the workflow system user id WF-BATCH.

c) The user(s) to whom the email notification is to be sent have the organizational plan attribute FORWARD_WI (Flag: Forward Work Item) set to "X" and have a valid email address assigned to their EBP user id. These can be checked via the standard EBP web transactions "Change Attributes" and "Change settings" respectively.

d) For EBP 2MB systems ensure OSS notes 354082 and 353746 have been applied (included in patch SAPKU2OBO8).

Program RSWUWFMLEC should be scheduled to run on a regular basis, e.g. once every 15 minutes. A user with appropriate authority must be assigned to the job. By preference this should be a generic batch ("System") user id with SAP ALL authority.

Assign the user id WF-BA TCH as the executor of the RS WUWFMLEC step.

Ensure the user id assigned to the job has an email address in their user master (otherwise you will get a transmission failure error, because the sender does not have an email address).

The parameter "One mail per work item" should be turned on to ensure the email contains details of the specific work item including a hyperlink to the workitem. The web server/port used in the hyperlink are taken from the organizational plan attribute ITS DEST (Current ITS of user).

The parameter "Protocol: Everything" should be turned on so that the number of mails sent successfully/unsuccessfully is written to the spool list (this is useful in tracking down problems).

Emails are only sent if there are outstanding workitem that have been created as of the last run date/time of the job. If the user touches the workitem prior to job execution, no mail will be sent.

Note that emails are never automatically deleted. It is up to the user to delete the email once it is no longer required.

Debugging of the email notification:

a) Check the user's organizational attributes using function module BBP GET ATTRIBUTES in test mode.

b) Use transactions SWU3 and/or SUO 1 to check that an email address has been assigned to the workflow system user id WF-BATCH.

c) Check that the RSWUWFMLEC job is running. Check any spool lists from the job. If there are no spool lists, no outstanding workitems were found. If the spool list indicates, "Transmission failed", most likely cause is a bad email address for user id WF-BATCH.

d) Use transaction SCOT to check that emails have been sent to the mail server correctly. The "Internal Trace" utility is useful to debug problems in sending the mail to the mail server. Emails in "Waiting" status can be pushed through to the mail server manually with the "Start send process" function. Emails in "In Transit" status have been sent to the mail server. Emails in "Error" status indicate a problem at the mail server.

e) Use transaction SOST to view each message sent and specific problems per message. This transaction also shows whether the message has been created but not yet sent to the mail server.

f) If there is a problem at the mail server, contact the mail server owner for assistance with tracing the email through the mail server.

g) If necessary, change the parameters "From work item creation date" and "From work item creation time" to recreate mails for outstanding workitems that have been previously processed by the RSWUWFMLEC program.

Question 44: What is a Meta-BAPI?

A: Each meta-BAPI is a function module beginning with META_*

Whenever calls to a backend system are involved, meta-BAPIs are used to determine and call the appropriate function module for the type of backend.

Meta-BAPIs are specific to a particular function, e.g. "Validate account assignment", "Create purchase order". These functions are also expressed as methods of objects, e.g. Purchase order object BUS2012, method "CreateFromData".

The meta-BAPI determines the type of the backend system (e.g. local, R3 version 3.1, R3 version 4.OB, R/3 version 4.5B, R/3 version 4.6A, non-R/3 system), and then reads the matching entry on table BBP_FUNCTION_MAP for the relevant object/method/backend type combination to find the backend specific function module to be called.

The backend specific function module exists in the EBP system. Its' purpose is to prepare and reformat data then call the relevant routine(s) for that backend type. All backend specific function modules for the same object /method have the same parameters, i.e. the meta-BAPI makes one dynamic function call and assumes that parameters are the same for all the function modules.

Question 45: What are some popular modifications or enhancements that are done to the SRM system?

A: Use of the catalog content BADI to reformat and/or map supplier specific values (such as product categories) to desired values.

Use of the catalog content BADI to reformat and/or map special fields in the. OCI (e.g. customer fields) to appropriate table/fields for further processing..

Modifications to the shopping cart creation transaction and associated services/templates to hide fields (e.g. to hide free text entry area), or to make new fields/screens available. E.g. tracking number.

Modifications to the shopping cart creation transaction and associated services/templates to change suggested defaults, e.g. default unit of measure, default catalogue

Modifications to the account assignment function group and associated services/templates to make new fields available. E.g. activity type.

Modifications to the shopping cart status transaction and associated service/templates changed to hide fields or to make new fields/screens available.

Use of the backend object determination BADI to reassign shopping cart items to desired backend object determination.

Use of backend object creation BADIs to prepare additional information for passing to the backend object, e.g. tracking number.

Modifications to the web transaction for shopping cart approval and associated service/templates to display additional information as part of the approval workitem.

Search helps using backend data, e.g. in the account assignment screen, permit a search on internal orders when the "order" account assignment category has been chosen.

Question 46: What is the purpose of a BADI?

A: Business Add-Ins are essentially a new form of user-exit. The BADI approach provides greater flexibility than the user-exit approach.

For instance, it is possible for several separate implementations of the BADI to exist in parallel (although only one implementation may be active at any one time). This is very useful when comparing the effect of using different source code within the BADI.

It is also possible to define multiple implementations of the BADI and use a filter to determine which implementation is executed at runtime depending on the runtime data involved.

BADI implementations can be accessed via the IMG or via transaction SE 18.

Use se19 to make modifications to your custom class implementation.

Each BADI has a definition name, e.g. BBP_CATALOG_TRANSFER. The essential part of the BADI is the interface and the associated method.

"Implementing" a BADI involves creating a class and associated method based on the interface and method specified in the BADI.

Implementation commences by pressing the execute icon in the IMG, or use menu path Implementation>

Create in SE 18. As part of implementation a new class based on the interface is automatically generated. You must provide a Z name for the new class.

On the "Interface" tab of the implementing class, you can see the interface, the implementing class and the method name.

Once the new class has been created you can then enter your source code in the method (double-click on the method name to enter the source code area). The source code of a BADI can include calls to function modules, select statements to database tables, code manipulating data, etc.

However to work with the method you must know the parameters of the method. To do this you need to look at the interface or implementing class (double-click on either from the "Interface" tab of the implementing class or BADI definition). In the interface or implementing class display, the available methods are listed, cursor position on the matching method name for your BADI and press the "Parameters" button to see the parameters and their reference types.

Note that as BADIs are coded using object-oriented principles ALL parameter tables are tables WITHOUT header line.

That is, to read them in the method you need to use explicit workareas. For example,

```
Data: catalog_wa like line of catalog_content.
Loop at catalog_content into catalog_wa.
Move catalog wa—description to
Endloop.
```

Question 47: How do you activate or deactivate a BADI?

A: Once the code has been entered, syntax checked and generated, the BADI must be activated. This happens in two places. First, while in the source code, the source code must be activated. Second, while in the implementing class, the implementing class must be activated.

Both source code and implementing class must be active before the system will use the BADI.

To deactivate a BADI, deactivate the implementing class is sufficient. There's no need to deactivate the source code.

Question 48: What are some limitations of BADIs?

A: The parameters of the BADI cannot be changed, i.e. you cannot add or remove parameters. Only the contents of the parameters can be changed.

The BADI is called from a program. It is not possible to change the point at which the BADI is called. It is not possible to access global data of the calling program.

To determine where the BADI is called, i.e. which is its' calling program, the implementing class display includes a "where-used list" button.

One popular, but ill-advised solution is to simply "break out" from the encapsulation of the BADI call to a customer function module. Simply create a function module that imports the needed objects and exports them back. In the context of a function module call, you can have access to any SAP or table data that you need without the restrictions of ABAP objects.

Question 49: What are BAPI Extensions?

A: BAPI Extensions allow additional information (e.g. customer specific) to be passed from the EBP system to the backend R3 system, e.g. when creating purchase requisitions or purchase orders. BAPI extensions are available in certain backend R/3 system releases (OSS notes for the particular BAPI must be checked to determine which releases/minimum hotpacks provide extensions to the desired BAPI).

The real benefit of this technique is that it allows additional data to be passed into the BAPI. This caters not only for customer fields, e.g. customer-specific fields in account assignment, but also existing standard SAP fields that are not included in the standard data for the BAPI.

In conjunction with BADIs and/or customer specific meta-BAPIs in the EBP system, BAPI extensions applied in the backend R3 system allow more data to be passed than is included in standard EBP.

For example, when passing customer specific account assignment data from EBP to the backend R3 system.

Using BAPI Extensions — BAPIPO_CREATE Example This describes the basic operation of extensions using BAPI_PO_CREATE (purchase order creation) as an example.

1. You must have applied the patch that includes the BAPI extensions for the desired BAPI. Descriptions of the extensions for the BAPI are usually found in OSS notes. For instance, OSS note 336589 for purchase orders, 336692 for purchase requisitions. Check the

notes carefully as the patches are spec j/ic and may only apply to certain R/3 releases.

2. The BAPI will include an EXTENSIONIN table parameter with structure BAPIPAREX. This parameter is used to pass the additional information into the target system (i.e. the system owning the BAPI). Note: There is an equivalent parameter for passing additional details to the source system, EXTENSIONOUT. You need to look at the specWc BAPI and relevant OSS notes to determine whether this parameter exists for the desired BAPI.

3. The first 30 characters (field STRUCTURE) of the EXTENSIONIN parameter is filled with the name of the structure used to define the format of the additional details, e.g. BAPI_TE_PO_ITEMS. After the structure name, the remaining fields are filled with the additional data in the matching format. A maximum of 960 bytes of data may be passed per EXTENSIONIN row not including the structure name. The 960 bytes of data are split across 4 fields of 240 bytes each — VALUEPARTI to VALUEPART4. You may add as many rows as necessary to the EXTENSIONIN table.

The structures used to define the format are known formats to the BAPI. For instance, BAPI_PO_CREATE allows structures BAPI_TE_PO_HEADER, BAPIJE_P0_ITEMS, and BAPI_TE_PO_ITEM_ACCOUNT to be used to pass additional header, item and account assignment details respectively.

5. Within the known structures, key information is held to match the additional data to the standard data. For instance, BAPI_TE_PO_ITEMS contains the purchase order item number to be matched to the standard item data passed to the BAPI in the table parameter P0_ITEMS.

6. After the key information, the required additional data is added. This may be done via a CI include if available, or via append structures. However it is vital that all fields included in the additional data must match be created with field names matching the target structures. The OSS note specific to the desired BAPI's extension will identify the target structure. For instance, the target structure for purchase order items is EKPO. So the addit ional data fields in BAPIJEPOJTEMS must have the same field names as their target fields in structure EKPO. Note: This may mean ignoring the usual naming convention of ZZ* for fields in append structures.

7. At runtime, after the standard data has been used to fill the target structures, the additional data in the EXTENSIONIN parameter is also used to fill the target structures. Note: This is usually done via a MOVE-CORRESPONDING — so there is no opportunity to manipulate the additional data at this point. However f the BAPI also contains user exits, they may allow some manipulation of the additional data prior to the MOVE-CORRESPONDING command.

Further Information

More information on this and related BAPI enhancement/extension techniques is found in SAPNET alias BAPI, in the "Developer's Guide" section for BAPIs.

Question 50: What is the Modification Assistant?

A: It is the SAP software that aids in the Process for applying modifications

You still require an object key from OSS. As in previous releases, this is usually requested when you first enter the program/screen/etc. in change mode.

In change mode, code/screen remains protected but new pushbuttons appear:

Insert — adding a block of code, adding screen elements (e.g. new fields) Replace — comments out existing code, gives a copy of existing code to modify Delete — comments out existing code — be careful that integrity of program is maintained, i.e. that it can still be successfully syntax checked and generated Remove modification — returns the program, etc. to SAP standard. Also removes the relevant link on the modification log.

The blocks are marked with:

- An opening comment line starting with *#{

- A closing comment line *#}

- When each new modification is made, once a change request is assigned to the object, the change request number is automatically included in the opening comment line.

How do I find existing modifications?

The modification log (transaction SE95) gives a breakdown and, in many cases, double-click access to modified objects. This is an excellent resource as an overall view of all the modifications in the system. It includes all modified objects even "safe" modifications such as append structures.

Question 51: What are some common upgrade issues?

A: Transaction SPDD and SPAU are still used to adjust the objects. However changes made via the modification assistant are analyzed at a fine granularity, e.g. the subroutine level. Automatic reapplication of modifications is available where SAP standard has not changed. Semi automatic reapplication of modifications is available where SAP standard has changed but it is still easily determined by the system where the modification belongs. In more complex situations, a split screen editor supports manual reapplication of modifications. The split screen editor allows identification, for example, of each individual modification block and the ability to opt to remove/copy to a nominated position/manually adjust code. The manual reapplication of modifications can be entered multiple times, and requires positive confirmation that all modifications in that object have been completed.

Limitations of modification assistant

Modification assistant is NOT used for ITS files such as services and templates. This means particular care must be taken to record all changes made to services and templates.

Modification assistant is NOT used for changes to messages classes and messages. Modification assistant is NOT used for changes to business object type programs.

Upgrade from 2.0 to 4.0 goes surprisingly smooth, with the exception of vendors. See section on debugging vendors for more specific information.

Question 52: What are some of the most important services in SRM?

A: Service GLOBAL holds the reference to the EBP system and the exit URL. Unless a specific exit URL is desired, default value of— should be the entry point, i.e. http://<EBPwebserver>:<EBPport>/scripts/wgate/bbpstart/!?—language=en

Service BBPGLOBAL holds all the shared MIME files, including shared HTMLBusiness function files, Javascript files and Java applet files.

Service BBPPU99 is the main shopping cart creation service.

Service BBPACCOUNT controls the account assignment display for a number of other services such as shopping cart creation, confirmation, invoices, etc.

Service BBPPUO2 is the shopping cart status service.

Service BBPCFO2 is the confirmation (i.e. goods receipt/service entry sheet) service.

Services starting with TS_TS* are services related to workflow workitems.

Standard system templates, scripts, HTMLBusiness function files, etc. are included in the templates directory under the "SYSTEM" service folder. This includes the workplace integration (WP1NTEGRATION), and search help (SEARCHHELP) files. All runtime ITS error message templates are also in the system folder.

Question 53: What are some of the issues surrounding making modifications to ITS service files and templates?

A: Modification assistant is NOT available for ITS service/template files. Version management is available for ITS service/template files but lacks certain functionality (temporary versions are ok, but patches tend to not to preserve the versioning). Therefore it is ESSENTIAL that changes to ITS service/template files are adequately recorded. Always make a backup copy of the file, ideally creating a separate file directory for the backup files.

To access the service/template files, from transaction SE8O, choose the object type "Internet Service" and enter/search for the appropriate Internet service name. Double- clicking on the service name itself accesses the service file. In the launch pad, expand the service to access the theme, expand the theme to access the templates. Double- clicking on the theme itself accesses the language resource file (if existing). Double- clicking on the template name accesses the template. When working with template files it is worthwhile using the "hide launchpad" button, as many of the files are greater than 80 characters across.

Multimedia files within a service are also accessible via transaction SE80 in the same way. However not all multimedia files can be viewed or modified via SE8O. Import/export of multimedia files is more likely.

Publishing ITS files

In transaction SE8O, choose menu options Utilities → Settings. Go to the ITS tab. Select the specific ITS from the drop-down list. If no ITS appear or the desired ITS does not appear this indicates that the IACOR NT service has not been configured and should be resolved with whichever Basis person is responsible for the ITS installation.

It is also possible to publish the files to a local file directory (e.g. for backup, for documentation purposes) by selecting that option and entering an appropriate directory.

NOTE: Publishing settings last for the duration of the logon session only.

To publish the files, display the relevant service in the launchpad, right-click on either the service or the particular file to access the "Publish" option on the context menu. When multiple files are to be published for the same service, right-click on the service and select "Publish..." → "Complete Service".

After publishing, the message "Object published successfully" should appear in the message line. Any problems/warnings should result in a dialog box appearing with a log list of objects attempted to be published and appropriate red/yellow/green icons indicating error/warning/success messages.

If the message "Application log could not be displayed" appears, this indicates that there is insufficient authority to show the log. This will only appear if there was an error/warning with the publishing. As warnings appear when new service/theme directories are created on the ITS, it is worthwhile publishing again in this case as a second publish should then return, "Object published successfully".

Special files to modify

Runtime ITS error messages need to be personalized for the company involved. Do this by changing the HEAD.html and TAIL.html templates in the "PM" productive mode) directory within the "SYSTEM" folder in the templates directory. Ensure the company's logo is included in HEAD.html template. Ensure references to the company's help desk are included in the TAIL.html template. Remove references to SAP AG and SAP logos in both templates.

Add the company logos to the start and home pages by replacing the following multimedia files within the BBPGLOBAL service, theme 99:

1. Company logo — LOGO.GIF in the IMAGES/START directory.

2. Main home page picture — BG START.jpg in the IMAGES/HOMEPAGE directory

3. Default photo picture (which user's can personalize) — DEFAULT_PHOTO.gif in the PHOTO directory.

Assessing Graphic dimensions

So that suitable logos/home page graphics can be chosen or created, it's useful to be able to assess the dimensions of these graphics.

The simplest way to do this is to open the graphic on it's own in the web browser screen, e.g. by URL http://<webserver>:<port>/sap/its/mimes/bbpglobal/99/images/start/logo.gif

Right-click on the graphic and go to "Properties" to find the dimensions in pixels. Remember that only pixels matter on web pages, as pixels are a measure relative to the screen resolution.

If an existing customer-specific graphic of different dimensions is to be used in place of the default graphics, it may be necessary to use a graphics program, e.g. Microsoft PhotoDraw, to adjust the dimensions of the customer-specific graphic so that it fits the EBP web page.

Question 54: How do you add a search help to the shopping cart?

A: Create a search-help in the usual way from the data dictionary (transaction SE11).

One possible difference with EBP is that the data to be selected may exist only in the backend system. To use data in the backend system, create the search-help without a selection method. Instead enter a search-help exit.

Attach the search-help to the relevant screen field via the screen field attributes, or to the data element of the relevant screen field.

Using a search-help exit to read backend data

Search-help exits are function modules. Create the function module by copying function module F4IF_SFILP_EXIT_EXAMPLE.

Add the search help type pool to the global data of the function group and any other data definitions needed to support the search help exit code.

Example:

Type-pools: SHLP.

Data: backend system like rfcdes—rfcdest, Backend destination washlpselopt like ddshselopt, "Selection options

order type type bapi2O75 2—order type, "Selection criteria order_list type standard table of bap120751. "Output list

To retrieve data from the backend R3 system, replace the section "STEP SELECT" with suitable code.

e.g.

If calicontrol-step = 'SELECT'.

*Determine the backend logical system, e.g. by reading table

BBPBACKENDDEST

*Read the search criteria — example below uses a parameter ORDER_TYPE

* created in the searchhelp

Loop at ship—selopt into washipselopt.

Case washlpselopt-shlpfield.

When 'ORDER TYPE'

If wa shlp selopt—sign = 'I'

And wa ship selopt-option = 'EQ

Order_type = washipselopt-low.

Endif.

Endcase.

Endloop.

*Retrieve the data from the backend R/3 system, e.g. via a suitable

BAP I

Call function 'BAPIINTERNALORDERGETLIST'

Destination backend system

Exporting

Order_type = order_type

Tables

```
Order_list        = order_list.
If sy—subrc ne 0.
Callcontrol—step = 'EXIT'.
Exit.
Endif.
*Format the data for the searchhelp Call function 'F4UT
RESULTS MAP' Tables
Shlp Tab          = ship_tab
Record_Tab        = record_tab
Source_Tab        = order_list
Changing
Ship      = shlp
Cailcontrol = cailcontrol
Exceptions
If sy—subrc = 0.
Cailcontrol—step = 'DISP'.
Else.
Calicontrol—step = 'EXIT'.
Endif.
Exit.
Endif.
```

Question 55: Is there anything in particular about transporting and change management in SRM?

A: Organizational plans and agent assignment are master data and should not be transported, but instead created in the appropriate system client.

Question 56: Is there an ITS or web service debugger?

A: Yes, there is an ITS debugger.

Debugging must be turned "ON" for the virtual ITS and a debugging port assigned.

This can be done via the admin service (i.e. remote administration of the ITS). The ITS must be restarted for these settings to take effect.

Question 57: How can you debug the build of a catalog URL?

A: Use ITS debugging to debug from the point of selecting the desired catalog and press the "Go" button. This invokes the ok-code CTLG in program SAPBBPPU99, which in turn calls function module BBP CALL CATALOG.

Question 58: What are some of the most common problems with vendors in SRM?

A: After vendor replication from the backend you will see dummy vendors in the org plan. Should you delete them? There are two philosophies:

It may happen that your shopping cart is getting stuck at err "Vendor XXXXXX is not intended for purchase org." In this case, go to the business partner administration view and ensure that the vendor is extended to the purchasing org to which the user is assigned.

Question 59: How can you debug an SRM workflow problem?

A: In particular the following program should be added to the EBP system:

Use BBP_PD to find work item number and SWI1 to trace workflow log.

Note that the final step in the approval workflow is to start the shopping cart transfer routine (function module BBP_REQREQTRANSFER). Problems in this routine can affect the approval status display on the web even if the workflow was executed successfully. In particular, if the shopping cart is still in "awaiting approval" status even though it has been approved via the workflow, this indicates that the BBP_REQREQTRANSFER routine was unable to complete processing of the shopping cart.

If BBP_REQREQ_TRANSFER has failed, messages should appear on the application monitors. It is also possible to debug the failure using transaction SE37 to run BBP_REQREQTRANSFER in test mode against the affected shopping cart.

Debugging Backend Object Choice

Create a shopping cart but HOLD (park) it, but don't order it.

Using transaction SE37 "Test" mode input the shopping cart number to function module BBP_REQREQTRANSFER and debug from that point.

Question 60: How can you debug the Initial Creation of a purchase order?

A: Create a shopping cart but place it on HOLD, do not order it. Debug from there.

Use BBP_PD to find work item number and SWI1 to trace workflow log. Use the function module builder, transaction se37, to execute function BBP_REQREQTRANSFER and debug from this point on.

Debugging Failure to Create a Backend Object

Use transaction SE16 with table REQREF to find the backend object type and backend object number reference for the shopping cart/item(s) involved.

Function modules:

<u>For earlier EBP versions</u>

SPOOL_REQ_CREATE_DO for purchase requisitions

SPOOL_PU_CREATE_DO for purchase orders

SPOOL_RS CREATE DO for reservations

<u>For EBP 4.0</u>

BBP_PO_SC_TRANSFER

BBP_PD_SC_RESUBMIT

Question 61: What are some of the Backend Object Types?

A: BUS2105 = Purchase requisition

BUS2012 = Purchase order

BUS2093 = Reservation

BUS2017 = Goods Receipt

Question 62: What does Shopping Cart Error: "Partner master data" or "invalid address" mean?

A: The address for the user's org unit may not have been maintained or inherited properly.

Run transaction CRM_OM_BP_INTEGRATE for the shopping cart creator's org unit. Check that an org unit address has been correctly created.

Use BBP_PD to find work item number and SWI1 to trace workflow log. Run transaction CRMM_BP for the shopping cart creator's contact person (i.e. Business Partner id assigned to the shopping cart creator). On the "Relationships" tab, drill down on the BTJRO1O ("is employee of") relationship to the org unit's business partner id. The org unit address should be displayed. If not, repeat these steps with CRPVIIM BP in "change" mode, and when drilled down on the org unit business partner, "Assign comp.address" to link the org unit address to the employee to org unit relationship.

Question 63: How can you check on an invoice?

A: Go to WE05 – IDOC processing

BD87 – If an IDOC is stuck, you can fix the error and re-process sometimes

Use BBP_PD to find work item number and SWI1 to trace workflow log.FB03 is display of purchasing docs.

Goto Display, and find the internal Invoice number from the CoCode, Fiscal Year, and Reference Key (the SRM doc number)

Question 64: Is there a way to ensure that a PO is issued to the preferred vendor?

A: Yes. Force the preferred vendor to fix vendor in the doc change BADI.

You can use method IF_EX_BBP_DOC_CHANGE_BADI~BBP_SC_CHANGE.

You will have to work with partner function '00000039' which is the preferred vendor to move it into partner function '00000019' which is the fixed vendor

In the BBP_DOC_CHANGE_BADI we provide the business partner data through the IT_PARTNER interface table. The prefered vendor or desired vendor has partner type 39. The regular supplier will have partner type 19. A switch from 39 to 19 should create a PO instead of requisition

Question 65: What is a service partner?

A: A service provider is a user created for a business partner.

When you go into business partner administration to create a contact person for a business partner you choose to create A) Contact Person OR B) Service Provider OR C) Both (by checking both check-boxes).

Question 66: How can you find SRM error message texts?

A: Table T100

Message class BBP_PD, BBP_WFL, etc.

Examples:

BBP_WFL 013, Approval workflow is ambiguous. Inform system administrator
BBP_PD 488, Current document status does not permit this action

Tax Jurisdiction code messages

Reference to Note: 650893 Message class TAX_TXJCD Customizable message

All that was required was to edit V_T100C and turn off message 105 for

TAX_TXJCD.

FM for vendor review: BBP_BUPA_XPRA_30A

Question 67: Is there anything you can check for errors during creation of the Org Plan?

A: Check the Business Partner address information – the address data was not included in the business partner creation. Could happen when you save an Org before adding the address.

You may need to run SE38:
CRM_MKTBP_ZCACL_UPDATE_30

Those orgs with the error may still need to have the address manually added in BP but all new Orgs should behave correctly.

Question 68: Can you use PCARDS in standard SRM?

A: In the standard delivery, it is not possible to enter procurement card as a payment method when using Enterprise Buyer implemented in a "classic" scenario. Since the shopping cart does not contain procurement card information, it is not possible to pass this information on to the backend documents such as purchase requisitions and purchase orders in a "classic" scenario.

Question 69: How can you manually update the status of a shopping cart?

A: You can manually/immediately update information in EBP documents, run:

SE37: BBP_REQREQ_TRANSFER (transfers doc to backend)

SE38: BBP_GET_STATUS_2 (Updates info into EBP)

SE37: RHOMATTRIBUTES_CONSISTENCY

Look for HRT5500 / 5505 table and repair this.

It is caused by large changes in the Org Structure and messes up the Db call for these org elements (like Pgroups and POrgs)

Question 70: How can you Fix a broken Org Structure or SRM User?

A: Organizational synchronization – Fix Orgs

Transaction: CRM_OM_BP_INTEGRATE

Users assign to Org, fixes users

Transaction: USERS_GEN

Maintain Attribute inheritance

Se37: T770MATTR

EBP Administrator via SAPGUI

Transaction: RZ20

Question 71: How can you Approve a shopping cart via SAPGUI?

A: Run transaction SE37: BBP_PDH_WFL_APPROVAL_SIMULATE

Enter BUS2121 and SC#

Copy Work Item Number (i.e. 25230)

SWI1: Enter WI# into Identification

Ensure Personal Settings have flagged

Enable forwarding to others

Use all objects

Technical views

Edit->Change

Complete manually (Status changed to "completed")

Also note SWI5 to view work item

You must have personal workflow settings indicate "technical view" – otherwise you cannot change the work item.

Question 72: How can you make HTML Changes to SRM services?

A: Transaction SE80. To help find the correct service, Run transaction in GUI, i.e. BBPSC01

If you can't run the transaction directly, make sure to type /n to exit any transaction. You can also try running the transaction via se93.

When you run BBPSC01, you can select technical details, and get technical info, template and screen name.

Another trick is to use the shopping cart from the web, find the field on the web page, and "View Source" by right clicking in the appropriate area. Take care that due to many sub-screens, you must click in just the right place to get the source code you may be going after.

Edit template: Internet Services (se80) for EBP – that contain the templates that we changed:

BBPSC01

BBPGLOBAL

BBPSEARCH

BBPACCOUNT

Remember to save and republish the templates after making changes

Question 73: What are some important transaction codes in SRM?

A: PPOMA_BPP, USERS_GEN, BBP_PD

The following is a comprehensive list of transactions available in the SRM 4.0 system.

BBP0	Start Menu for SAP B2B Procurement
BBPADDREXT	Maintain Vendor Address - External
BBPADDRINTC	Maintain Addresses for Own Company
BBPADDRINTV	Maintain Vendor Address (Internal)
BBPADM_COCKPIT	Administrator Monitor Dummy
BBPADM_MONITOR	FlowLogic Service BBPADM_MONITOR
BBPAPPL	Define EBP Applications
BBPAPPL_DISP	Define EBP Applications
BBPAPPL_TRSP	Define EBP Applications
BBPAT02	Parameter ID tree maintenance
BBPAT03	Create User
BBPAT04	Forgotten User ID/Password
BBPAT05	Change User Data
BBPATTRMAINT	Maintain Attributes
BBPAVLMAINT	AVL Maintenance (Display / Change)
BBPBC1	XML invoice transfer
BBPBWSC1	SC Analyses for Manager (Old)
BBPBWSP	Start Enterprise Buyer Inbox

BBPBWSP_SIMPLE	Start Enterprise Buyer Inbox
BBPCACC	Maintain Account Assign. Categories
BBPCF01	GR/SE for Vendor
BBPCF02	GR/SE for Desktop User
BBPCF03	Goods Recpt/Serv.for Profession.Use
BBPCF04	Confirmation Approval
BBPCF05	Carry Out Review for Confirmation
BBPCMSG1	Customizing Flexible Message Contr
BBPCMSG2	XML Message Control
BBPCTOL	Maintain Tolerences
BBPCU04	Set Up Default Workflows
BBPCU05	Link Manager to Org. Structure
BBPCU06	Link Administrator to Org. Structure
BBPCU07	Current Role for User Generation
BBPCU08	Workflow Wizard
BBPDIFF	Version Comparison
BBPGETVD	Transfer Vendor Master
BBPGLOBAL	Transaction for Internet Transaction
BBPHELP	Help for Specific Transactions
BBPINSTALLCOUNTRIES	Activate country-specific EBP field
BBPINSTALLSZENARIO	Installation of CUF Scenarios
BBPIV01	Vendor User Invoice Input
BBPIV02	Desktop User Invoice Input

BBPIV03	Prof. User Invoice Input
BBPIV04	Invoice Approval
BBPIV05	Perform Invoice Review
BBPIV06	Change Incorrect XML Invoice
BBPMAINAPP	Startup for Vendor Approval
BBPMAINEXT	Process Vendor or Bidder
BBPMAININT	Process Vendor or Bidder
BBPMAINMANAGER	Process own Company (only)
BBPMAINNEW	Request Vendor or Bidder
BBPMAINPURCH	Process own Purch.Org. View (only)
BBPMONSTART	Start the BBP monitors
BBPOR01	Component Planning for Orders
BBPOR02	Postprocessing Orders
BBPPCO01	PCO: Prof. User
BBPPCO02	Purchase Order Response: Entered By
BBPPCO_PO	Purchase Order Confirmation: Call P
BBPPCO_WF	Purchase Order Confirmation: Call W
BBPPO01	Purchaser Cockpit
BBPPS01	Component Planning for Projects
BBPPS02	Postprocessing Projects
BBPPU07	Manager Inbox
BBPPU08	Employee Inbox
BBPPU09	Administrator Cockpit
BBPPU12	Reviewer Inbox
BBPRP01	Reporting, Data Retrieval from Core
BBPSC01	Shopping Cart - Full Functionality
BBPSC02	Shopping Cart - Wizard
BBPSC03	Shopping Cart - Limited Functions
BBPSC04	Shopping Cart Status
BBPSC05	Public Template (Create)
BBPSC06	Public Template (Change)
BBPSC07	Manager Inbox
BBPSC08	Employee Inbox

BBPSC09	Administrator Cockpit
BBPSC10	Reviewer Inbox
BBPSC11	Shopping Cart Display Item Overviev
BBPSC12	Shopping Cart Display Item Details
BBPSC13	Change Shopping Cart
BBPSC14	SC Display for Rec. Mangagement
BBPSC15	SC Display for CFolder
BBPSC16	SC Number of Itm Det. for CFolder
BBPSC17	SC Number of Itm Det. for Rec. Mgn
BBPSC18	Request Temporary Staff
BBPSC19	Request External Staff (Change)
BBPSHOWVD	Display vendor data
BBPSOCO01	Sourcing Cockpit
BBPSR01	Service Entry (Component)
BBPSR02	Entry Sheet Maintenance (Compone
BBPST01	Start EBR Menu
BBPST02	Start EBR Menu
BBPSTART1	FlowLogic Service BBPSTART
BBPSUBSCRIBE	Add additional subscriber user data
BBPTRACE	Switch on EBP Trace
BBPTRACK	Status Tracking: Call Structure
BBPUPDVD	Update Vendor Master Record
BBPUSERMAINT	user Maintain
BBPU_IAC_TEST	Test Transaction for ITS
BBPVE01	Vendor Evaluation
BBPVENDOR	BBP Vendor Logon
BBPWEBMONITOR	Application Monitor w/o Flow Logic
BBPWEBMON_SEP	Monitor in New Window
BBPWI	Central Initial Screen WI Execution
BBPWLRA01	Workload Reassignment
BBP_ARCH_RESI	Define EBP Residence Times
BBP_ATTR_CHECK	EBP Organizational Model: Checks
BBP_AUCTION	BBP Live Auction
BBP_AUC_SRM_EX	Live Auction Return from Applet

BBP_BE_LIST	Vendor List
BBP_BGRD_APPROVAL	Background Approval
BBP_BID_EVAL	EBP Bid Evaluation
BBP_BID_EXTSO	Display Bid Invitation from SOCO
BBP_BID_INV	BBP Bid Invitation Cockpit
BBP_BP_OM_INTEGRA TE	Integration BP Orgmanagement
BBP_BW_SC2	SB Monitoring Admin (PD)
BBP_BW_SC3	Shopping Carts per Product
BBP_BW_SC4	Shopping Carts per Cost Center
BBP_CCM_TRANSFER	Data Transfer to Catalog
BBP_CFOLDER	Redirect from cFolders
BBP_CHECK_USERS	Check EBP Users
BBP_CLEANER	Start Synchronization with Backend
BBP_CND_CHECK	Check Conditions Customizing
BBP_CND_CHECK_CUS T	Check Conditions Customizing
BBP_CONT_ACTION_D EF	Define Action Profiles
BBP_CTR_DISP	Contract in Display Mode
BBP_CTR_DISPNR	Display Contract without Return
BBP_CTR_EXT_PO	Display Contract from PO and SOC
BBP_CTR_EXT_WF	Display Contract from Workflow
BBP_CTR_MAIN	Process Contracts
BBP_CTR_MAINCC	Process Global Outline Agreement
BBP_CTR_MON	Monitor Contract Distribution
BBP_CTR_SEARCC	Find Global Outline Agreement
BBP_CTR_WF_APP	Branch from Approval Workflow
BBP_CTR_WF_CHG	Branch Contract from Change Workfl
BBP_CT_SCM_STAGIN G	Staging UI for Schema Import
BBP_CT_STAGING	Staging
BBP_CUST_CAT	Call Structure Maint. of Catalogs
BBP_CUST_DET_ACCT	Determine G/L Account by Category

BBP_CUST_DET_LOGSYS	Determine Target System by Catego
BBP_CUST_LOGSYS	Maintenance of the Backend System
BBP_CUST_TARGET_OBJ	MMaint. of Objects to Be Generated
BBP_CUS_ACCESS_SEQ	EBP: Define Access Sequences
BBP_DYN_ATTR_EDIT	Maintenance of Dynamic Attributes
BBP_EVAL_SURVEY	Survey Cockpit
BBP_GETCD_ITS	Display Change Documents
BBP_MON	Open the Monitor Display
BBP_MON_SC	Monitor Shopping Cart
BBP_MS_ACC_DET_C	Multiple Company: Acct for Category
BBP_MS_BE_C	Multiple Company:Maintain FI Backe
BBP_MS_MAP_TAX_C	Multiple Company: Tax Code
BBP_MS_MSG1_C	Message Control
BBP_MS_MSG2_C	Multiple Company: Flex. Message X
BBP_MS_STD_ACC_C	MultipleCompany:LocalAcctAssigmtD
BBP_NUM_AUC	Number Range Maintenance 'AUC'
BBP_NUM_AVL	Number Range Definition 'AVL'
BBP_NUM_BID	Bid Invitation Nr Range Maintenance
BBP_NUM_CONF	Procure. Confirm. Nr Range Mainten.
BBP_NUM_INV	Invoice Number Range Maintenance
BBP_NUM_INVD	Number Ranges for Invoice Templat
BBP_NUM_PC	No.Range Maint. Contrct/Del.Schedu
BBP_NUM_PCO	Number Range Maint for NkObj POC
BBP_NUM_PO	Purchase Order Nr Range Maintenan
BBP_NUM_QUOT	Bid Number Range Maintenance
BBP_NUM_SUSASN	Number Range Maintenance: 'SUSAS
BBP_NUM_SUSCF	Number Ranges Maintenance: 'SUSF
BBP_NUM_SUSINV	Number Ranges for 'SUSINV'
BBP_NUM_SUSPCO	Number Ranges for 'SUSPCO'
BBP_NUM_SUSPO	Number Ranges Maintenance: 'SUSF
BBP_OCI_AGENT	Cross-Catalog Search

BBP_OM_TRANSL	Translate Organizational Units
BBP_PCCOM	PCard Commitment Customizing
BBP_PD	Document Display (EBP)
BBP_PDH_TEXT	bbp_pdh_text
BBP_PD_PO_ERRORLOG	Starts Entry Screen for Error Log
BBP_PM01	Postman scenario
BBP_POC	Process Purchase Orders
BBP_POC_DISPLY	Display Transaction for the PO
BBP_POC_WF_APP	Approval Transaction for the PO
BBP_POC_WF_REQ	Approval PO for Requester
BBP_POC_WF_REV	Approval PO for Reviewer
BBP_PO_ACTION_CONF	Configure Action Conditions
BBP_PO_ACTION_DEF	Define Action Profiles
BBP_PPF	Output Control Purchase Order
BBP_PPF_CONT	Trigger Selection Contracts
BBP_PPF_OLD	PO Trigger Administration
BBP_PRODUCT_SETTING	BBP with/without CRM
BBP_QUOT	Create Bid
BBP_QUOT_EXTST	Display Bid from Status
BBP_QUOT_EXTWF	Display Bid Invitation -> Bid fr. WF
BBP_SC_DARKAPP_IAC	Approve Shopping Cart in Background
BBP_SNEW_SYNCVD	Shows New Vendor Repl. from Backend
BBP_SP_COMP_INI	Replication of Companies & Employees
BBP_SP_SUPP_INI	Download Vendors for Service Portal
BBP_SUPP_MONI	Vendor Monitor
BBP_SUS_BP_ADM	Management of Business Partners
BBP_TRIGG	Output Actions
BBP_TRIGG_CTR	Output Contract
BBP_TRIGG_ERS	Output ERS Document
BBP_TRIGG_INV	Output Invoice
BBP_TRIGG_MEN	Output Document

Question 74: Is there anything we should know about change management or transporting objects in SRM?

A: SRM is a different sort of beast than R/3. Here's one concrete reason why. SRM is different because there are dozens of critical configuration and development items that are client and system specific, and as such are non-transportable. I've seen large enterprises struggle to keep any sort of change management systems in place with the SRM product, and they have suffered in maintenance. The mistake here is not to validate that all configuration and development artifacts are kept consistent throughout your system landscape for each and every change. It's a mistake to keep different org plans in DEV, QA, and PROD, and it's a mistake to have to test your code in production after you've gone live.

The change management strategy should account for one very important difference in all SRM implementations – the client specific configuration that needs to be completed for each system. It is a mistake to set your consultants off configuring, and not keep tabs on DEV, QA, and PRODUCTION. SRM can require a fair amount of client-specific configuration and master data maintenance. You should devise a plan and make an employee responsible for keeping each system and client in synch. Pay careful attention to your org plan. It makes sense to put one person in charge of the org plan, and also make that person responsible for keeping and changing each applicable system.

Making something a priority in your implementation means that your resources have enough time to do things the right way. Make sure there is enough time built into your plan to come up with and enforce a proper change management process.

Question 75: **Why is it a good idea to try and use external catalogs?**

A: One of the most forward-thinking capabilities of the SAP SRM system is also one of the most overlooked. Allowing your vendors to maintain a special view of their catalog for use by you and only you can save your company mountains of work in keeping vendor catalogs coherent with current pricing. Not letting your vendors maintain their own data is a mistake.

Start early and decide on several key vendors to form preferred relationships with. You will negotiate a contract with each vendor. One particularly successful SRM implementation offloaded the quite considerable master data maintenance task associated with maintaining an internal catalog to about a dozen key external vendors who agreed to maintain external catalogs.

INDEX

ABOUT THE AUTHOR

Jim Stewart (Los Angeles, CA) is the author of the popular "SAP SRM Advanced EBP Cookbook" and has over 10 years of experience as an information systems professional, during which time he has served as a technical analyst, lead developer, and functional team lead. He has implemented SAP at The US Army, Raytheon, General Mills, and other Fortune 100 clients. Mr. Stewart is the founder of Equity Technology Group, an SAP consulting partner, and continues to practice as a consultant in the area of SAP SRM/EBP, Workflow, Web programming, and UNIX systems administration.

www.ingramcontent.com/pod-product-compliance
Ingram Content Group UK Ltd.
Pitfield, Milton Keynes, MK11 3LW, UK
UKHW040032200726
13854UKWH00001B/486

9 780975 305218